GETTING TO KNOW
THE U.S. PRESIDENTS

R I C H A R D M.
NIXON

THIRTY-SEVENTH PRESIDENT
1969 – 1974

WRITTEN AND ILLUSTRATED BY MIKE VENEZIA

CHILDREN'S PRESS
AN IMPRINT OF SCHOLASTIC INC.
NEW YORK   TORONTO   LONDON   AUCKLAND   SYDNEY
MEXICO CITY   NEW DELHI   HONG KONG
DANBURY, CONNECTICUT

Reading Consultant: Nanci R. Vargus, Ed.D., Assistant Professor, School of Education, University of Indianapolis

Historical Consultant: Marc J. Selverstone, Ph.D., Assistant Professor, Miller Center of Public Affairs, University of Virginia

Photographs © 2007: Alamy Images/POPPERFOTO: 9; AP/Wide World Photos: 32 (Bob Daughtery), 14; Corbis Images: 22, 26, 30 (Bettmann), 19 (David J. & Janice L. Frent Collection), 8 (Wally McNamee), 5 bottom right; Getty Images: 10 (Hulton Archive), 27 (Bob Peterson/Time Life Pictures), 25 (Pictorial Parade/Hulton Archive), 24 (Howard Sochurek/Time Life Pictures), 5 bottom center (Stock Montage/Hulton Archive), 3 (The White House/Hulton Archive), 23 (Time Life Pictures), 5 top center (Washington/AFP); Index Stock Imagery/Stock Montage: 5 top right; IPN Stock Images/Dennis Brack: 4; North Wind Picture Archives: 5 bottom left; Robertstock.com: 17; Steve Wolowina: 28; The Image Works/Richard Ellis: 5 top left.

Colorist for illustrations: Andrew Day

Library of Congress Cataloging-in-Publication Data

Venezia, Mike.
  Richard M. Nixon / written and illustrated by Mike Venezia.
    p. cm. — (Getting to know the U.S. Presidents)
  ISBN-13: 978-0-516-22641-5 (lib. bdg.)   978-0-531-17949-9 (pbk.)
  ISBN-10: 0-516-22641-X (lib. bdg.)   0-531-17949-4 (pbk.)
  1. Nixon, Richard M. (Richard Milhous), 1913-1994—Juvenile literature
2. Presidents—United States—Biography—Juvenile literature. I.
Title. II. Series.

  E856.V46 2007
  973.924092—dc22
  [B]

                            2006023350

1 2 3 4 5 6 7 8 9 10 R 17 16 15 14 13 12 11 10 09 08   62

President
Richard M. Nixon

R ichard Milhous Nixon was the thirty-seventh president of the United States of America. He was born in Yorba Linda, California, in 1913. Richard Nixon could have been remembered as a great president, except for one thing. He was caught lying and trying to cover up illegal things he had done. Because of this, President Nixon was forced to resign.

What's the big deal? You guys all had scandals, too.

The event that led to Richard Nixon's resignation was known as the Watergate scandal. A scandal is a disgraceful event that damages someone's reputation. Many other presidents were involved in scandals, but none were ever forced to resign.

Clockwise from left: John Adams, Bill Clinton, Ronald Reagan (with a chimpanzee who starred with him in a movie before he was president), Ulysses S. Grant, Warren G. Harding, Thomas Jefferson

Watergate was the name of a fancy hotel and group of office buildings in Washington, D.C. The Democratic Party had its headquarters there. While Nixon was president, on June 17, 1972, five mysterious burglars were caught breaking into the headquarters. It was soon discovered that the burglars were actually members of a committee to reelect President Nixon.

The five Republican burglars were planting tiny electronic listening devices called "bugs" to spy on the Democrats and learn about their plans during the 1972 election year. By 1972, spies around the world had perfected these devices to listen in on and record phone conversations. Before this time, it was difficult to hide a recording machine that no one would notice.

The Watergate burglary led to an investigation of President Nixon and his closest advisors. It was discovered that they were involved in illegal wiretapping. They had also spied on private citizens, bribed people to keep their mouths shut, and lied to cover up their activities.

Before the Watergate scandal was discovered and even while it was being investigated, President Nixon accomplished many important things. He traveled to the People's Republic of China. China was a Communist country that had been an enemy of the United States. President Nixon and Chinese leaders agreed that it was time for both countries to start getting along better.

Chinese Premier Zhou Enlai (left) and President Richard M. Nixon (right)

President Nixon shakes hands with Soviet leader Leonid Brezhnev

President Nixon then traveled to another enemy country, the Soviet Union. He got its leaders to agree to limit the making of missiles that carried nuclear weapons. At home, President Nixon had started the Environmental Protection Agency. This agency helped control pollution, so U.S. citizens would have cleaner air and water. President Nixon also worked hard to finally end the Vietnam War.

President Nixon grew up in a hardworking family. He had one older brother and three younger brothers. All the Nixon kids worked hard to help the family businesses.

Richard Nixon (back left) at age nine with three of his brothers

Frank Nixon, Richard's father, owned a
lemon orchard in Yorba Linda, but the orchard
didn't do very well. The Nixons hardly had
enough money for food and clothing. Mr. Nixon
finally had to sell the orchard and try to find
another job.

When Richard Nixon was nine years old, his family moved to Whittier, California. In Whittier, Frank Nixon opened up a gas station and grocery store.

When Richard was old enough, he would get up every morning at 4:00 a.m. and drive to Los Angeles to pick up fresh fruits and vegetables for the grocery store. Even with his heavy workload, Richard did well in high school. He sometimes studied all night to get good grades. Richard wanted to please his parents more than anything.

In high school, Richard Nixon showed a special talent for debating and writing compositions. He even won a scholarship to Harvard University in Massachusetts. Richard didn't end up going to Harvard, though. His family didn't have enough money to pay for his travel and living expenses. Richard decided to go to nearby Whittier College instead. After he graduated, Richard saved enough money to attend law school on scholarship at Duke University in North Carolina.

Dick Nixon was a second-string football player at Whittier College.

Richard Nixon got his law degree at Duke, returned home, and joined a law firm. Soon, Richard began to think about following a dream he had. He had always wanted to get into politics. Richard joined local groups and clubs, hoping to meet and impress as many important people as possible. He hoped that someday these people might vote for him.

Richard Nixon also joined a theater group. Dick, as he was often called, was considered a pretty good actor. It was during a play rehearsal that he fell in love with his co-star, a girl named Pat Ryan. For Dick, it was love at first sight.

Pat and Richard Nixon with their daughters

It took Pat a little longer to get used to Dick, though. After dating for two years, Pat and Dick decided to get married. They had two daughters, Tricia and Julie.

Soon after Dick and Pat got married, the United States entered World War II. Dick Nixon joined the U.S. Navy. He wasn't sent into combat, and ended up spending a lot of time playing poker. Dick made quite a bit of money playing cards in his spare time.

When the war ended in 1945, Dick returned home, ready to get back to Pat and his law business. Members of the local Republican Party had a different idea in mind for Dick, though. They wanted him to run for the U.S. House of Representatives.

Dick couldn't wait! He used the money he had won playing poker to pay for his campaign. He worked harder than ever to beat the Democratic nominee and became a U.S. Representative in 1947. Then, just three years later, Richard Nixon decided to run for the U.S. Senate. He won that race, too.

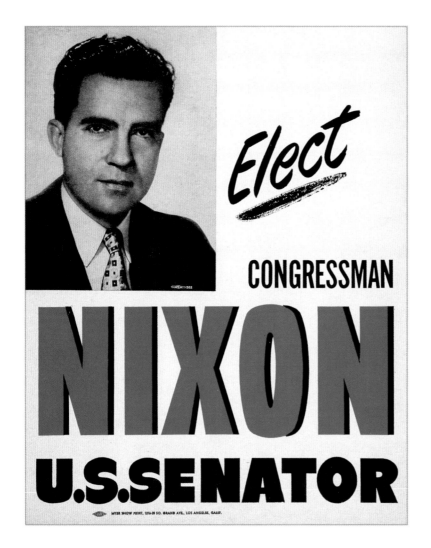

A Nixon U.S. Senate campaign poster

During this time, many people feared that Communism might take over the country. Richard Nixon used the threat of Communism to help him win his elections to Congress.

Communism is a system where the government controls or owns land, factories, and other businesses. Their idea is to make sure everyone shares wealth equally, so there are no poor people or rich people. Communist governments are tough on their citizens, and usually end up taking away human rights.

Some people in the United States liked the idea of sharing wealth. Most people, though, saw Communist countries, like the Soviet Union, as being cruel and totally against freedom.

Richard Nixon hated the idea of Communism. He believed the candidates he ran against might be supporters of the Communist system. Richard Nixon cleverly accused his opponents of supporting Communism. The opponents denied it, but the voters ended up believing Nixon.

Congressman Nixon made a name for himself as someone who could protect the United States from Communist spies. Richard Nixon became a member of a group called the House Un-American Activities Committee, or H.U.A.C. This group investigated people who were sometimes found to be a danger to the United States. Unfortunately, many innocent people were accused as well.

Nixon (right) studies government documents during the investigation of accused spy Alger Hiss.

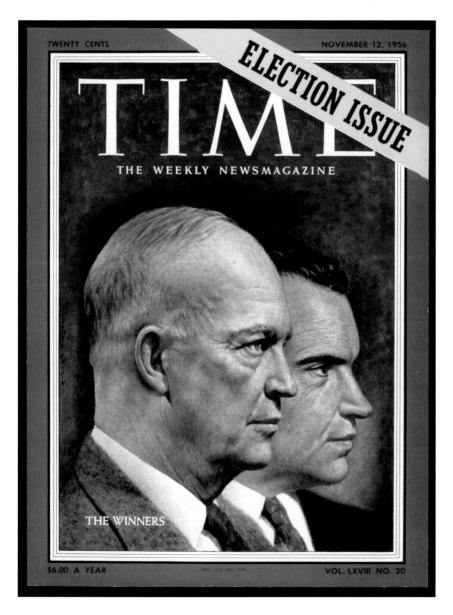

This was the cover of *Time* magazine the week after Eisenhower and Nixon won the presidential election of 1952.

In 1952, the popular General Dwight D. Eisenhower ran for president. Eisenhower had heard about the ambitious Richard Nixon and asked him to be his running mate. Eisenhower and Nixon won the election. In just six years, Richard Nixon went from being an unknown lawyer to vice president of the United States!

When Vice President Nixon visited the Soviet Union, he got into a heated argument with Soviet Premier Nikita Khrushchev (second from left, pointing) about whose country had better technology. This exchange became known as the "kitchen debate."

Richard Nixon turned out to be an excellent vice president. Once, when President Eisenhower became seriously ill, Vice President Nixon did a great job running the country for a while. As President Eisenhower's second term came to an end, Republican Party members thought Richard Nixon would be a good choice to run for president.

Millions of people watched the Nixon-Kennedy debates on television.

Nixon ran against the Democratic candidate, John Kennedy. It was a super-close race, but Kennedy won. A disappointed Dick Nixon returned to California. Two years later, he ran for governor of his state. Nixon lost that election, too. Angrily, he told newspaper reporters he was through with politics forever!

Richard Nixon may have been a poor loser, but he soon got over it. When the election of 1968 came up, Richard Nixon decided to run for president again! It was a restless time in the United States. African Americans were marching for their civil rights. Sometimes their demonstrations turned violent.

In April 1968, race riots broke out and buildings burned in several American cities after civil-rights leader Dr. Martin Luther King Jr. was assassinated.

Richard Nixon and his family celebrating his election to the presidency in 1968

American soldiers were fighting in an unpopular war in Vietnam, too. Richard Nixon promised he would bring peace with honor in Vietnam and law and order at home. He put all his efforts into the election, and this time he won!

President Nixon worked with Congress to create
laws to help make air cleaner in American cities.

Richard Nixon started out as a popular
president. He went to work right away
helping to create the Environmental
Protection Agency and the Endangered
Species Act. He also took steps to get along
better with China and Russia.

Richard Nixon was the first president to visit China. Pat Nixon went on the trip, too. She was a helpful partner to her husband. Chinese Premier Zhou Enlai liked Pat so much he gave her two rare giant pandas to bring back to the United States.

This photograph from 1970 shows hundreds of thousands of young people standing outside the White House to protest the war in Vietnam.

Things didn't go well for long, though. Even though President Nixon finally worked out a plan to bring troops home from Vietnam, it took much longer than people could stand. In fact, the war started to spread into nearby Asian countries. At home, more and more violent anti-war demonstrations broke out across the nation.

Soon, the Watergate scandal began to get more attention. At first, President Nixon denied having done anything wrong. Then it was discovered he had secretly tape-recorded conversations in his office. The Supreme Court ordered Nixon to hand over his tapes to investigators. The tapes proved that President Nixon did know about wrongdoing, and even approved it. Now the president was at risk of being thrown out of office! Richard Nixon couldn't face the possibility of being removed from office for criminal activities. Instead, he decided to resign on August 8, 1974, before his second term ended.

President Richard Nixon says goodbye after resigning from office in August 1974.

The next day, Vice President Gerald Ford became president. Even though Richard Nixon left his job in disgrace, he was an important historical figure. He continued to have a busy life, giving speeches, writing books, and meeting with government leaders. Nixon never had to worry about going to trial for his crimes. President Ford gave him a full pardon. Richard Nixon did have to live with his worst crime, though, letting down the people of the United States. Richard Nixon died in 1994 at the age of eighty-one.